CHARLIE PARKER FOR PIANO Book ONE

15 PIANO SOLOS — ARRANGED FROM HIS RECORDED SOLOS

*ARRANGEMENTS BY
PAUL SMITH AND
MORRIS FELDMAN (*)*

NTENTS

Photo Courtesy Polydor Inc.

My Little Suede Shoes

Piano Solo arranged by
Paul Smith

By CHARLIE PARKER
(Based on Charlie Parker Recording)
VERVE 8010
VERVE 2515

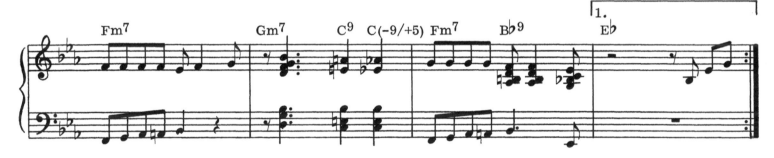

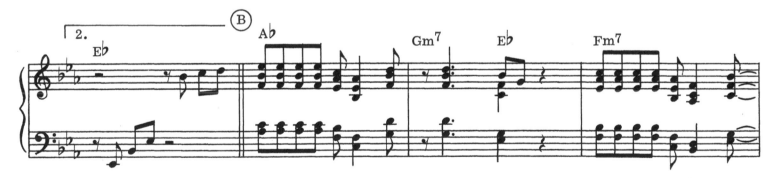

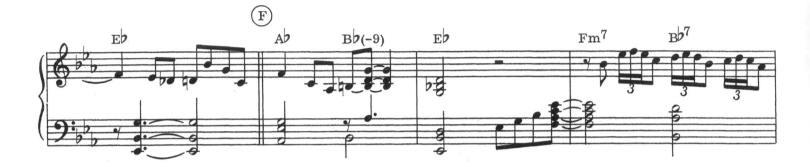

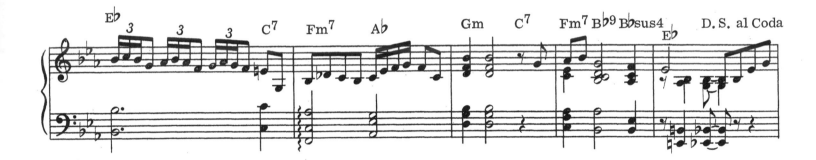

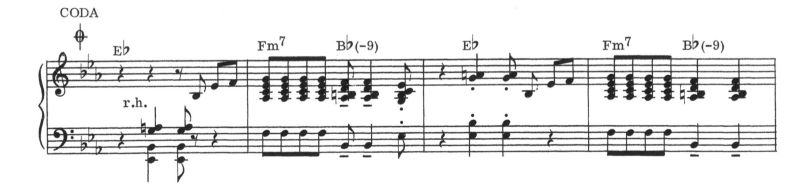

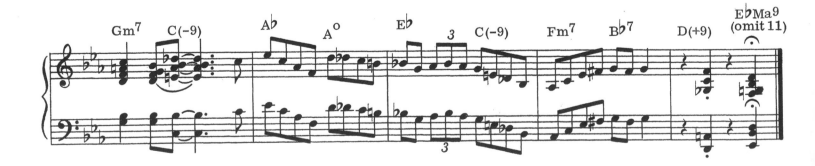

Segment

Piano Solo arranged by
Paul Smith

By CHARLIE PARKER
(Based on Charlie Parker Recording)
VERVE 8009

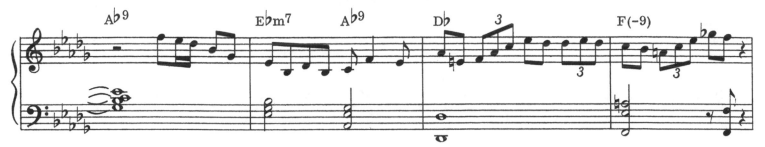

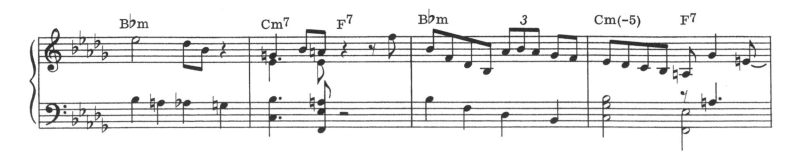

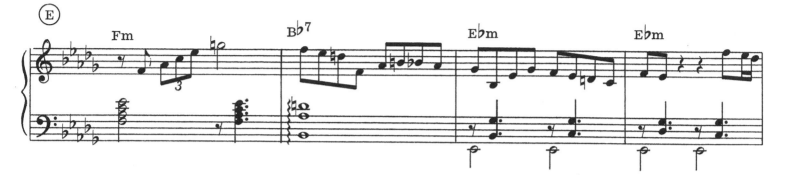

The Bird

**Piano Solo arranged by
Paul Smith**

By CHARLIE PARKER
(Based on Charlie Parker Recording)
VERVE 2501

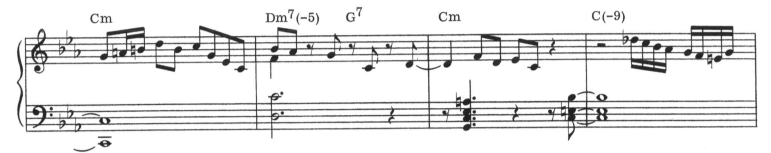

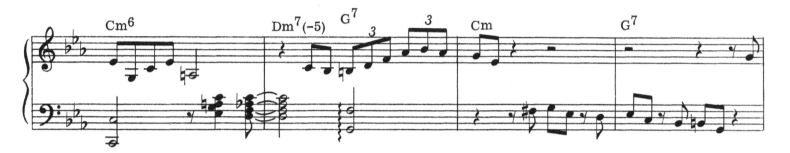

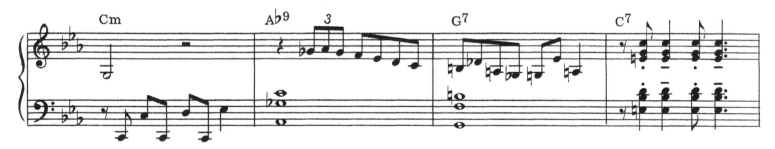

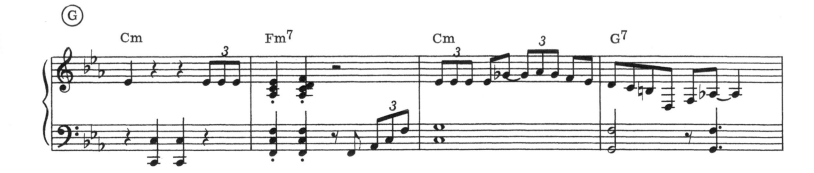

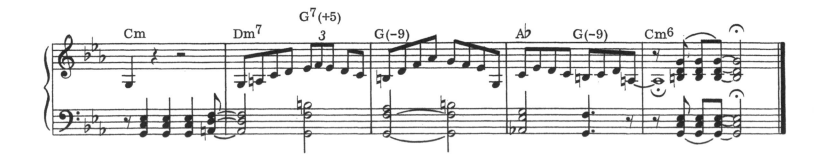

**Piano Solo arranged by
Paul Smith**

Blues for Alice

By **CHARLIE PARKER**
(Based on Charlie Parker Recording)
VERVE 8010
VERVE 2515

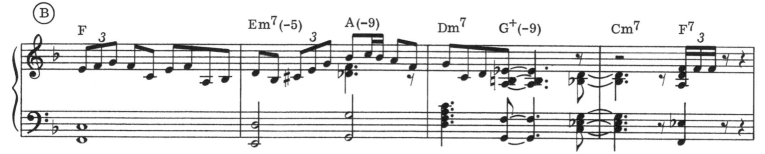

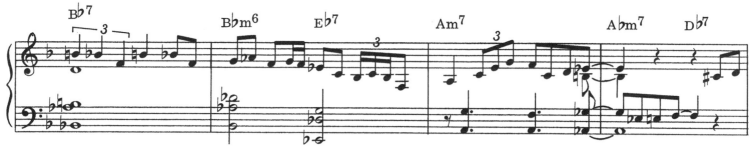

An Oscar for Treadwell

Piano Solo arranged by
Paul Smith

By CHARLIE PARKER
(Based on Charlie Parker Recording)
VERVE 8002
VERVE 8006
VERVE 2501

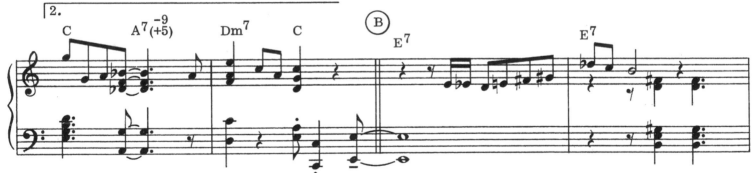

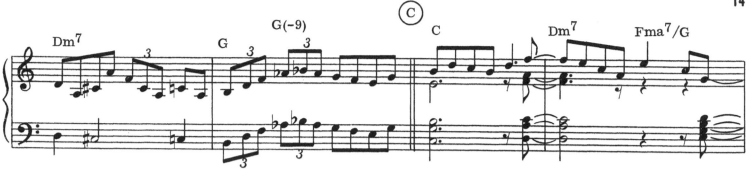

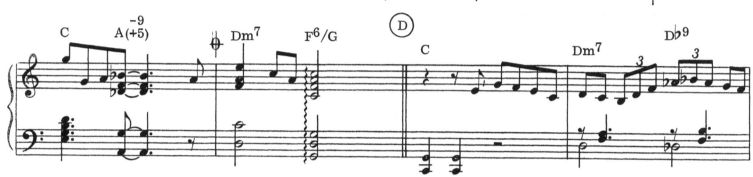

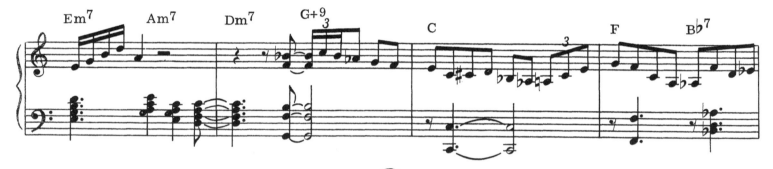

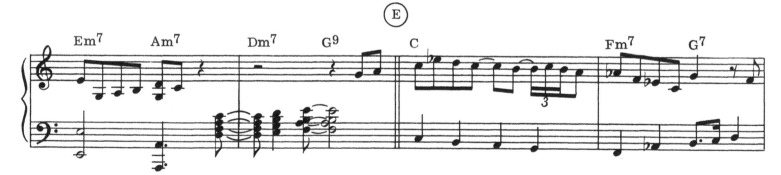

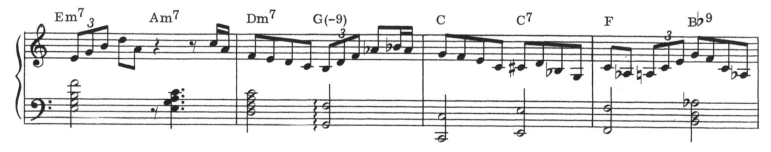

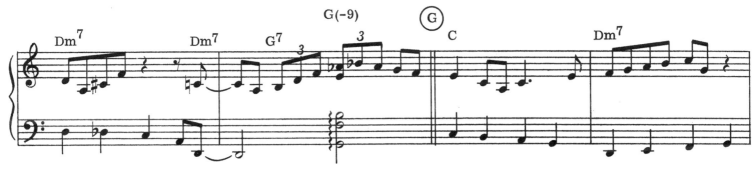

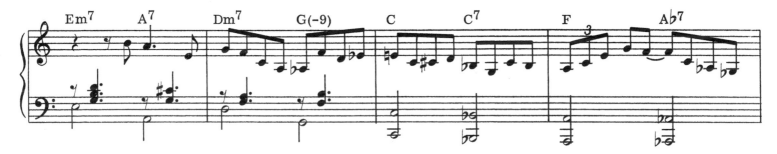

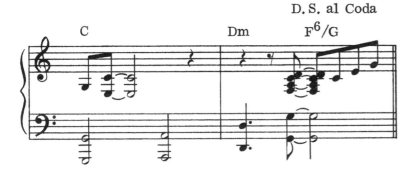

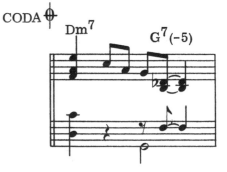

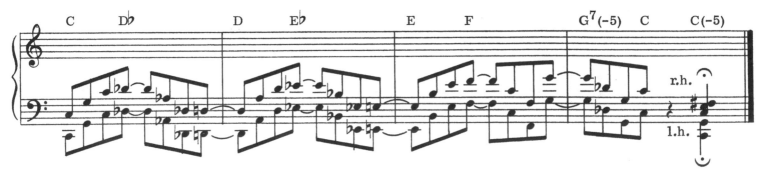

Kim

Piano Solo arranged by
Paul Smith

By CHARLIE PARKER
(Based on Charlie Parker Recording)
VERVE 8005
MGM 4949

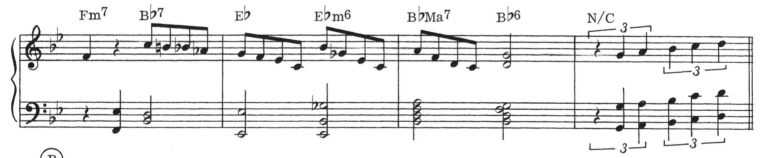

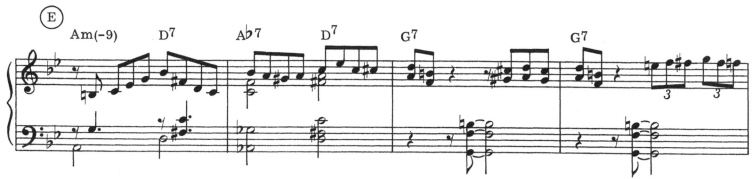

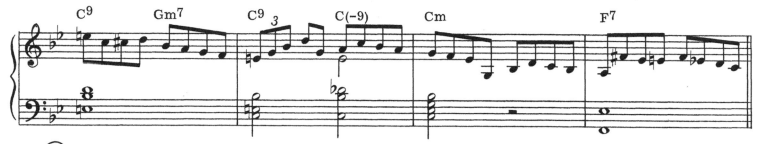

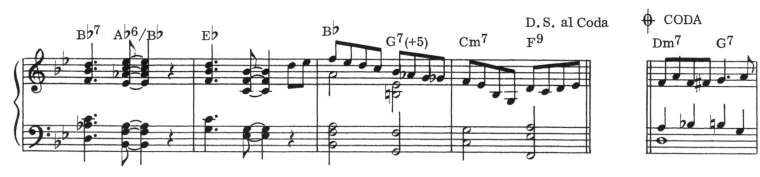

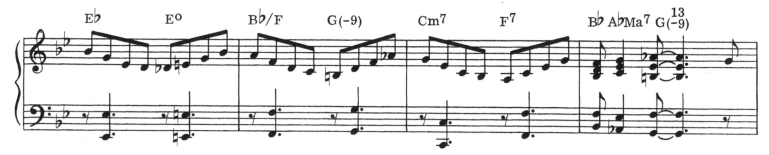

Back Home Blues

Piano Solo arranged by
Paul Smith

By **CHARLIE PARKER**
(Based on Charlie Parker Recording)
VERVE 8840
VERVE 8010
VERVE 2515

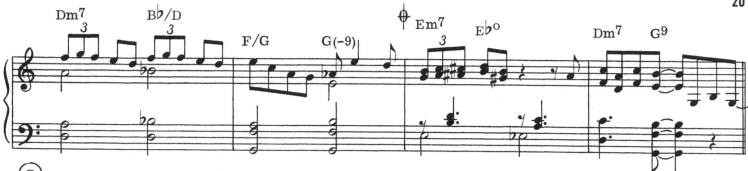

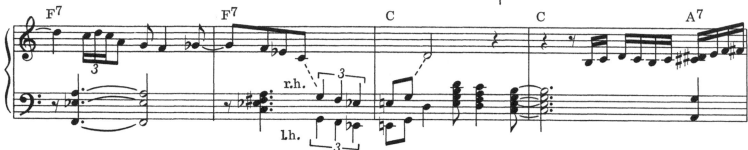

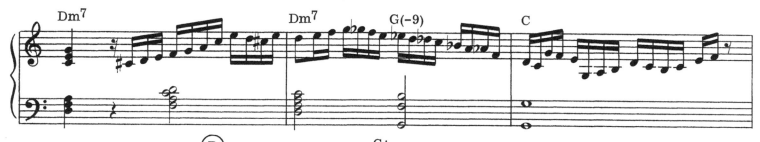

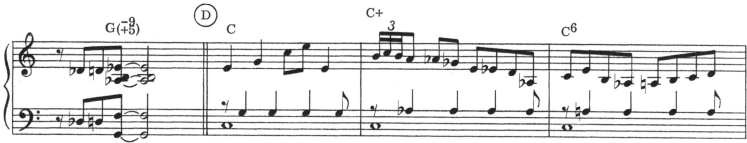

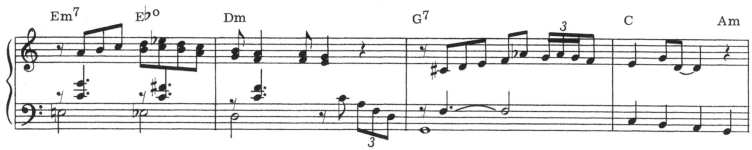

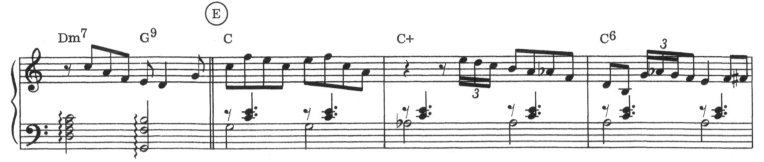

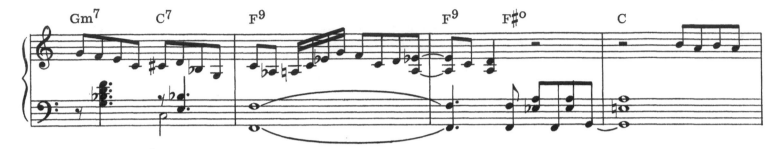

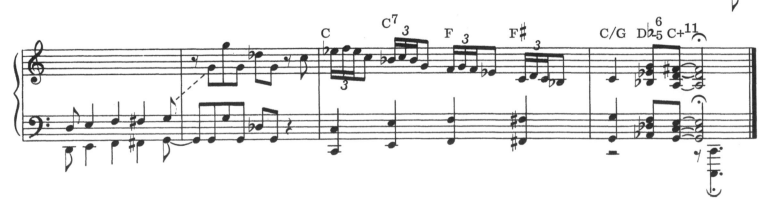

Au Privave

Piano Solo arranged by
Paul Smith

By CHARLIE PARKER
(Based on Charlie Parker Recording)
VERVE 8010
VERVE 4949
VERVE 2515

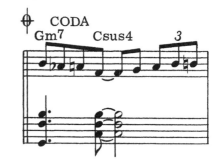

Piano Solo arranged by
Paul Smith

Visa

By **CHARLIE PARKER**
(Based on Charlie Parker Recording)
VERVE 8009 VERVE 8000

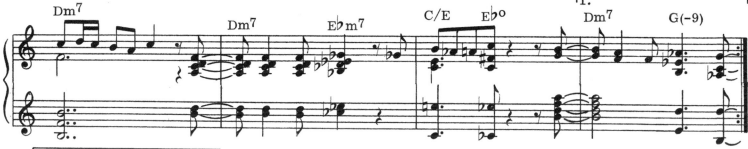

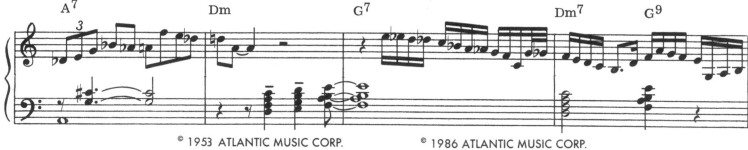

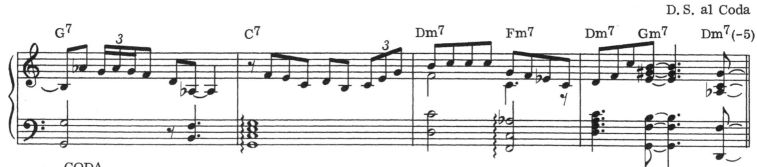

Chi Chi

Piano Solo arranged by
Paul Smith

By CHARLIE PARKER
(Based on Charlie Parker Recording)
VERVE 8005
MGM 4949
VERVE 8409

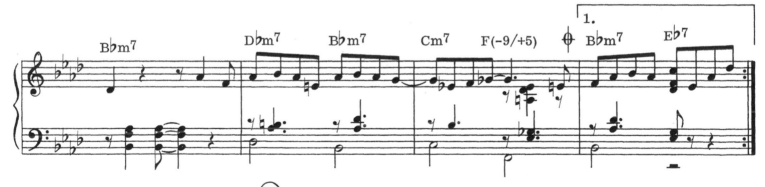

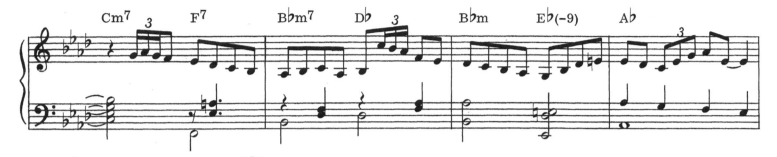

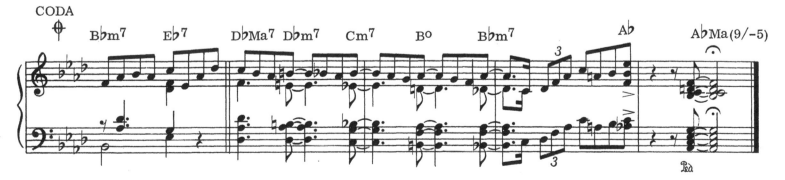

Ornithology

Piano Solo arranged by
Morris Feldman

By **CHARLIE PARKER** and **BENNIE HARRIS**
(Based on Charlie Parker Recording)
VERVE 407

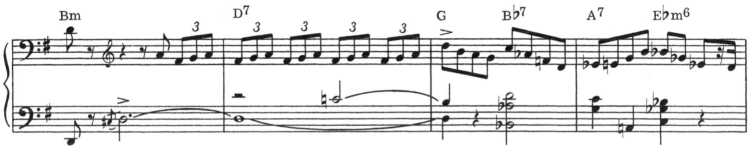

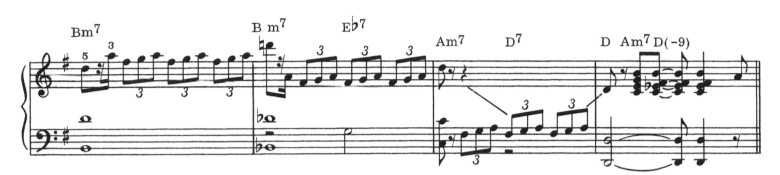

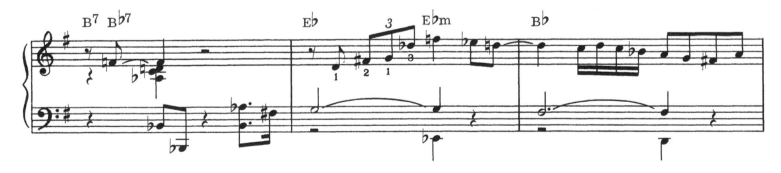

Moose The Mooche

Piano Solo arranged by
Morris Feldman

By CHARLIE PARKER
(Based on Charlie Parker Recording)
DIAL 1003B
Charlie Parker 407

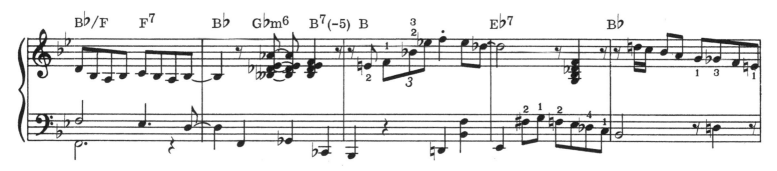

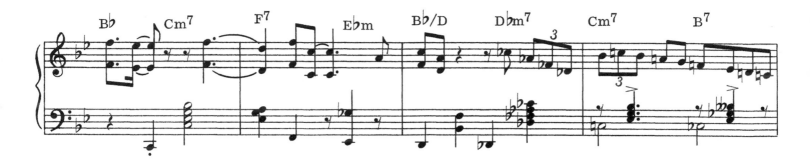

Confirmation

Piano Solo arranged by
Morris Feldman

By CHARLIE PARKER
(Based on Dizzy Gillespie Recording)
DIAL 1008A
VERVE 407

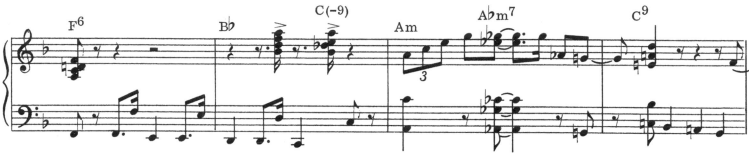

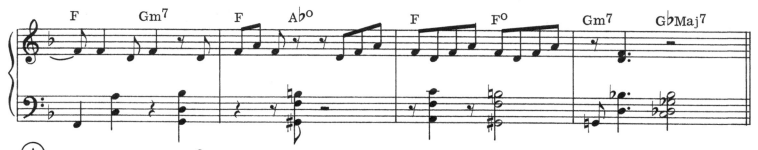

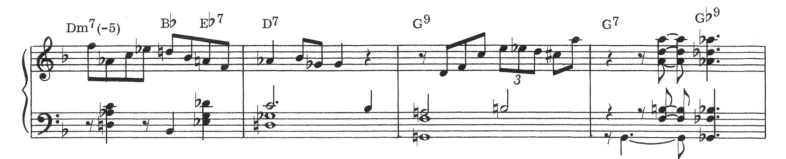

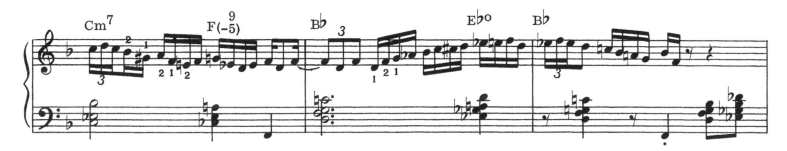

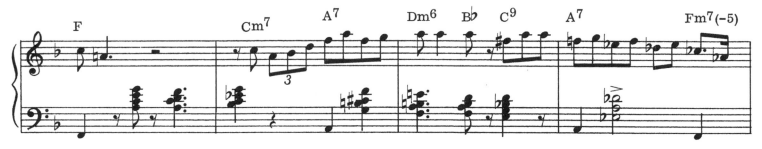

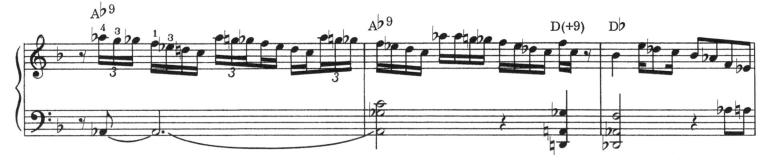

Yardbird Suite

Piano Solo arranged by
Morris Feldman

By **CHARLIE PARKER**
(Based on Charlie Parker Recording)
VERVE 407

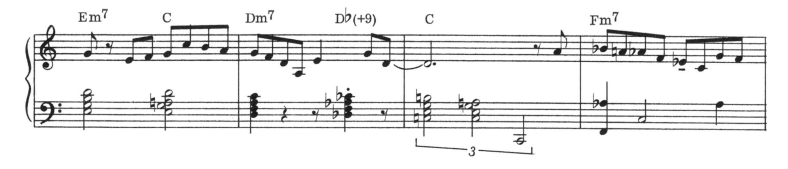

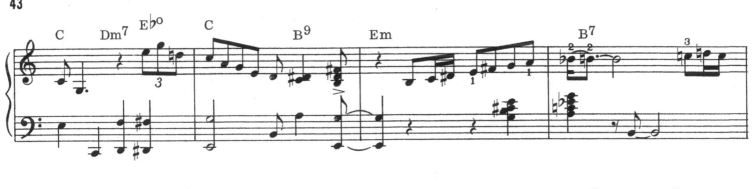

Card Board

Piano Solo arranged by
Paul Smith

By CHARLIE PARKER
(Based on Charlie Parker Recording)
VERVE 2501

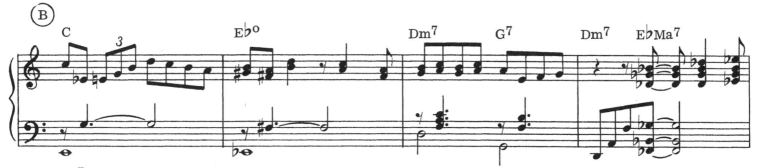

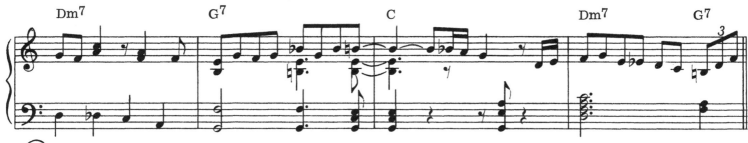

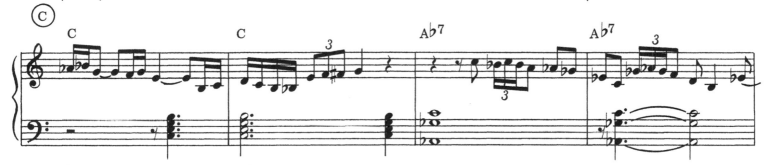

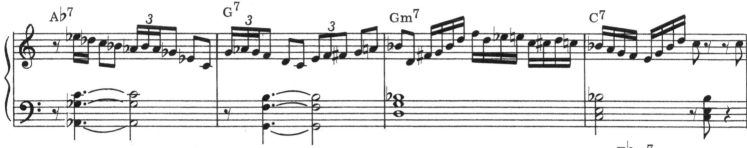

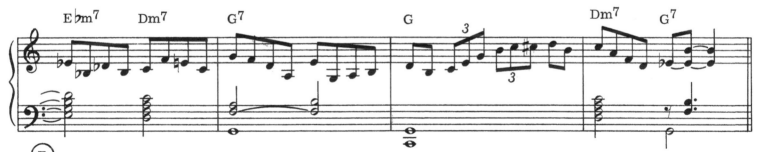